POPE LEO XIV

POPE LEO XIV

First American Pope

Liz Sonneborn

LERNER PUBLICATIONS ◆ MINNEAPOLIS

Lerner Publications Company
An imprint of Lerner Publishing Group, Inc.
241 First Avenue North
Minneapolis, MN 55401 USA

For reading levels and more information, look up this title at www.lernerbooks.com.

Main body text set in Rotis Serif Std 55 Regular. Typeface provided by Adobe Systems.

Editor: Brianna Kaiser **Photo Editor:** Cynthia Zemlicka

Library of Congress Cataloging-in-Publication Data

The Cataloging-in-Publication Data for *Pope Leo XIV: First American Pope* is on file at the Library of Congress.
ISBN 979-8-3480-4122-9 (lib. bdg.)
ISBN 979-8-3480-4123-6 (pbk.)
ISBN 979-8-3480-4124-3 (epub)

Manufactured in the United States of America
1-1012789-60012-7/11/2025

TABLE OF CONTENTS

Pope Leo XIV offers his first Regina Coeli prayer from St. Peter's Basilica on May 11, 2025.

On May 8, 2025, a crowd of forty thousand people waited in St. Peter's Square in Vatican City. Many of them had been there for hours under the afternoon sun. They hoped to witness an important event in world history. Every now and then, they scanned the roof of the Sistine Chapel for smoke. But all they saw there were seagulls resting in the sunshine.

Then a little after six o'clock in the evening, a burst of white smoke suddenly rose high in the sky from the chimney on the chapel's roof. The crowd erupted with cheers and applause. The bells of St. Peter's Basilica, a church in St. Peter's Square, rang out.

On May 8, 2025, white smoke coming up from the Sistine Chapel's chimney signals that a new pope has been chosen.

"Viva il papa!" people shouted in Italian. The phrase meant, "Long live the pope!"

Seventeen days earlier, Pope Francis had died at the age of eighty-eight. The pope is the leader of the Catholic Church. The religion Catholicism has a more than two thousand-year-old history. Like other Christians, Catholics follow the biblical teachings of Jesus, who they consider the son of God.

After Pope Francis's death, Catholics everywhere wondered who would become the new pope. The College of Cardinals, the body of all the cardinals in the Church, would make that decision. Cardinals are Catholic clergymen the pope chooses to serve as his closest advisers.

To vote on which cardinal would become the next pope, 133 cardinals came together at the Vatican, the Church's headquarters in Italy. On the evening of Wednesday, May 7, they entered the Sistine Chapel for the conclave, a gathering of cardinals to select the new pope. The doors closed behind them. They would not be allowed to have any contact with the outside world until they made their decision.

Cardinals hold conclaves in the Sistine Chapel.

The voting was done according to centuries-old rules. With each vote, the cardinals wrote their choice on a paper card. They tried to disguise their handwriting so that no one knew how they voted. To be elected pope, the candidate had to receive two-thirds of the votes. If no one received that many on the first round, the cardinals held more rounds of voting until someone reached two-thirds of the votes.

After the votes were counted, the ballots were burned in a stove connected to a chimney on the Sistine Chapel's roof. Church officials used chemicals to color the smoke from the burning pieces of paper. Black smoke told the world that the cardinals had not yet reached a decision. White smoke communicated that they had chosen a new pope.

On the second day of the conclave, after four rounds of votes, the crowd outside in St. Peter's Square finally spied the white smoke they had been waiting for. Everyone grew even more restless as they awaited the news of who the conclave had picked. Soon the doors opened on the basilica's balcony. Cardinal Dominique Mamberti emerged.

"Habemus Papam," Mamberti said in Latin. "We have a Pope."

The crowd renewed their cheers, almost drowning out Mamberti's announcement that the new father of the Church was Robert Francis Prevost. The cardinals had just elected the first pope from the United States. Prevost would take the name Pope Leo XIV.

A crowd in St. Peter's Square on May 8, 2025, waiting to hear who is the new pope

The cheering resumed louder than ever when Pope Leo XIV stepped onto the balcony. He was dressed in traditional red-and-gold papal regalia. The sixty-nine-year-old man with glasses and white hair wore a gentle smile as he choked back tears. He waved to the crowd.

Speaking in Italian, he uttered his first words as pope: "Peace be with you all."

The newly elected Pope Leo XIV greets a crowd from the balcony of St. Peter's Basilica on May 8, 2025.

The moment held great meaning for Catholics around the world. Many were overjoyed by their first glimpse of the man who would lead their Church into the future. And for Pope Leo XIV, the event was life-changing. He had entered the conclave as a cardinal, an important official of his beloved Church. He had left it as the 267th pope, one of the world's most influential and respected religious leaders.

Vatican City

Vatican City is an independent nation-state that lies in the middle of the city of Rome, Italy. With a population of about eight hundred people and an area of only 0.17 square miles (0.44 sq. km), it is the smallest nation in the world. Vatican City has its own government, which is overseen by the pope, and diplomats to establish formal relationships with other countries. Vatican City does not levy taxes and instead depends on donations from Catholic supporters to fund its operations.

Son of Chicago

On September 14, 1955, Robert Francis Prevost was born at Mercy Hospital in the South Side of Chicago, Illinois. He grew up just outside of Chicago in the working-class suburb of Dolton. The family's modest brick house had just enough room for him, his parents, and his two older brothers, Louis Jr. and John.

Robert's father, Louis Prevost, was of French and Italian heritage. After serving in the navy during World War II (1939–1945), he worked as a school superintendent. Robert's mother, Mildred Prevost, was descended from Creole people of color, who likely had African, Caribbean, and European roots. She was a librarian and had a master's degree in education.

Robert Francis Prevost (*left*) with his brothers Louis and John

Much of the Prevosts' family life was centered on their local Catholic church, St. Mary of the Assumption. The church ran the elementary school that Robert and his brothers went to. Each Sunday his family sat in the same pew for Mass. During this religious service, Catholic clergymen called priests perform Holy Communion. They give church members wafers to eat and sips of wine to honor Jesus's Last Supper.

The Prevost family was active in church life. Louis helped teach young people Catholic beliefs. Mildred created a library at St. Mary's and often sang in church. Robert was an altar boy who assisted priests during Mass. He also sang in the church choir.

Robert's brothers liked to play cops and robbers, but he preferred another game of make-believe. He pretended to be a priest. He used an ironing board as an altar and handed out candy in his own version of Communion. In and out of church, Robert seemed more religious than many of his St. Mary's classmates.

"We used to tease him all the time—you're going to be the pope one day," his brother Louis said. "Neighbors said the same thing."

After graduating from St. Mary's, most of Robert's friends went to local Catholic high schools. But Robert chose to leave his family to attend St. Augustine Seminary High School in Holland, Michigan. The religious boarding school prepared its young male students to join the priesthood one day. Priests of the Augustinian Order ran the school.

In the Catholic Church, an order is a community of people, such as priests or nuns, who have taken religious vows and live and observe their faith together. The Augustinian Order is much smaller compared to other Catholic orders such as the Franciscans and the Jesuits. In 2025 it had fewer than three thousand members worldwide. The order focuses on community and equality among its members. It also emphasizes missionary work—sharing their religious beliefs in another region or culture—and service to others.

St. Augustine

The Augustinian Order, also known as the Order of St. Augustine, was created in 1244. It takes its name and core beliefs from St. Augustine. He was born in present-day Algeria, a country in North Africa, in 354. A great philosopher and writer, he wrote the book *The City of God*, which helped shape modern Christian beliefs. St. Augustine is known as the doctor of the Church because of the importance of his writings to the Catholic faith.

A 1600s painting of St. Augustine by French artist Philippe de Champaigne

An excellent student, Robert sang in his school's choir, edited the yearbook, and performed skits with an acting club. For many St. Augustine students, the high school experience was difficult. Some got homesick and returned to their families. Others were overwhelmed by the religious training or had doubts about joining the priesthood, which required a lifelong commitment to serving the Church. Out of his class of several dozen students, Robert was one of only thirteen to graduate from the school.

Preparing for the Priesthood

Prevost continued his education at Villanova University. It was a top Catholic university near Philadelphia, Pennsylvania. The Augustinian Order ran it.

Prevost lived in a dormitory with other students who planned to become priests. The tight-knit group talked about current events through the lens of their faith. One topic was abortion, which had recently been legalized in the United States. In line with the teachings of the Catholic Church, Prevost opposed abortion. With some friends, he founded Villanovans for Life—the oldest college antiabortion group in the country.

The aspiring priests at Villanova also discussed new ideas in Catholic thought, including liberation theology. It explored the ways the teachings of Jesus could apply to real-world problems. Liberation theology became popular

Prevost graduated from Villanova University in 1977.

in Latin America, the Spanish-speaking areas within North and South America.

Prevost excelled at his studies, which focused on mathematics and philosophy. He took classes in Hebrew so he could read the Hebrew Bible. He also studied Latin, the ancient Roman language that priests used during Mass when he was a child. Knowing this language later helped him learn to speak Spanish and Italian. Both languages are rooted in Latin.

Prevost also used his time at Villanova to think hard about whether he really wanted to be a priest. Priests were not permitted to have romantic relationships or get married. Prevost confided to his father that he might want to marry and have a family. His father assured him that his deep love of God could also be fulfilling.

An older priest also offered Prevost some important advice. He told Prevost that not being able to have romantic relationships would be difficult when he was young. But as he got older, his real challenge would be obedience. The Church had a strict hierarchy of leaders, with officials such as bishops, cardinals, and the pope at the top. As a priest, he would be expected to obey higher-ranking Church leaders whether he wanted to or not.

By the time Prevost graduated, he was confident in his calling to the priesthood. He lived in an Augustinian community in St. Louis, Missouri, before returning to Chicago. Then he studied for a master's degree in divinity at the Catholic Theological Union.

After he graduated, Prevost headed to Rome. In June 1982 he became ordained as a priest. He moved into the Augustinian headquarters of St. Monica, which was across the street from St. Peter's Basilica. At St. Monica, he settled into the Augustinian style of communal living. He shared lodging and meals and sometimes played tennis, his favorite sport, with his fellow priests.

Prevost also began working toward a doctorate degree at the Pontifical University of St. Thomas Aquinas. He studied canon law, the body of laws under which the Catholic Church operates. Prevost worked on improving his Italian language skills too. He used Italian novels and television shows as study aids. By 1985 his long years of study ended, and he was eager to put his Catholic beliefs about serving others into practice.

Seeing the World

In 1985 Prevost traveled to South America to work as a missionary in Chulucanas, Peru. After a little more than a year, he went back to Chicago to work briefly at the Province of Our Mother of Good Counsel. This branch of the Augustinian Order is also known as the Midwest Augustinians.

In 1988 Prevost returned to Peru. This time, he settled in Trujillo, the third-largest city in the country. Trujillo would be his home for the next ten years. He quickly came to love Peru's tall mountains, its dense jungles, its pristine beaches and, most of all, its people.

An aerial view of the main square in Trujillo, Peru

Father Ramiro Castillo holds up a photo showing Prevost during his time in Trujillo.

Prevost took on a variety of roles in Trujillo. He was the priest of a local parish and taught young men looking to enter the priesthood. He also was a professor of canon law and a judge on a religious court that settled disputes between church members. Prevost became a beloved figure, especially among the economically disadvantaged, to whom he often provided food and shelter.

Prevost worked hard to keep the people of Trujillo safe during a violent time. A guerrilla group called the

Shining Path was battling the government and terrorizing many Peruvians. The group carried out bombings and assassinations. They also often targeted Catholic priests and nuns. Prevost was under constant threat of being kidnapped or killed.

The government forces that were fighting the Shining Path were also responsible for many cruel acts. Peru was under the control of a dictator who often ordered the murder of its citizens. Once when Prevost was traveling with a group of his students, heavily armed government soldiers stopped and boarded their bus. The soldiers wanted to force the students to join the army. Prevost confronted them, insisting that by law, young men entering the priesthood were exempt from military duty. The soldiers lowered their guns and let Prevost and his students continue on their way.

In 1999 Prevost was called back to Chicago to head the Midwest Augustinians. Two years later, Prevost was elected to lead the entire Augustinian Order. He headed to Rome and settled back into St. Monica, where he had lived as a doctoral student. For the next twelve years, he spent most of his time on the road.

Prevost traveled around the world and visited Augustinian priests and communities. He discussed important issues, such as poverty and abuse within the Church, with Augustinians of many different cultures. Listening and learning, he became a skilled diplomat. Prevost was becoming a respected Church leader across the globe.

Catholics Across the Globe

With 1.4 billion followers around the world, Catholicism is the largest Christian religion. According to a 2025 Vatican report, almost half of all Catholics (48 percent) live in North and South America. Catholics are also found in Africa (20 percent), Europe (20 percent), Asia (11 percent), and Oceania (1 percent). In 2025 about fifty-three million adults in the United States, around 20 percent of the country's adult population, identified as Catholic.

In Chiclayo

During his travels, Prevost sometimes visited Buenos Aires, the capital city of Argentina. Cardinal Archbishop Jorge Mario Bergoglio led the Church there. Prevost and Bergoglio became close friends. In 2013 Pope Benedict XVI resigned, and the College of Cardinals selected Bergoglio to be the new pope.

Taking the name Pope Francis, he was an unexpected choice. He was the first pope ever from South America. Pope Francis was eager to reform the Church to better serve the economically disadvantaged and migrants. Prevost largely supported Pope Francis's goals. But they also argued about small matters.

In 2013 Prevost planned to return to the United States after serving twelve years as the head of the

Pope Francis (*left*) meeting with Prevost in 2017

Augustinians. But Pope Francis had other plans for his friend. The next year, the pope sent Prevost back to Peru to lead the Church in and around the coastal city of Chiclayo.

Pope Francis made Prevost a bishop in 2015. As a bishop in the country, Prevost was required to become a citizen according to Peruvian law. Prevost got dual citizenship in Peru and the United States.

Prevost was happy to be back in Peru. He quickly won the affection of the people of Chiclayo by embracing local customs and going to cultural festivals and other public events. He became known for his quiet strength and pleasant nature. "No matter how many problems he has, he maintains good humor and joy," his friend and colleague the Reverend Fidel Purisaca Vigil said.

As he had in Trujillo, Prevost worked hard to help the economically disadvantaged of Chiclayo. He opened a soup kitchen and started a program to fight child hunger. He often drove his white pickup truck high into the Andes Mountains to bring food and other supplies to communities in need. Prevost also tried to help Venezuelan migrants. More than one million of them had come to Peru between the late 2010s and the early 2020s to escape the economic collapse of their own country.

Coming Under Fire

In 2000 a Chicago priest who had been accused of abusing several children went to live in a local Augustinian monastery, a building that housed a community of Catholic monks. The monastery was down the road from an elementary school. The *Chicago Sun-Times* reported on the incident in 2021. Prevost came under fire for putting the school's students in harm's way by allowing the accused priest to live nearby. The Church defended Prevost and said he had followed all Church rules in place at the time.

Prevost leads a Mass in Peru in 2018.

In early 2023 Pope Francis asked Prevost to return to Rome. At a gathering just before he left Peru, Prevost admitted that he had mixed feelings about the move. He had told the pope he would prefer to stay in Chiclayo. But his obedience to the Church left him with little choice but to accept the pope's new role for him.

Selecting Bishops

Prevost arrived in Rome in early 2023 to serve as the head of the Dicastery for Bishops. He became in charge of selecting and managing bishops around the world. It was one of the most influential posts in the Vatican. The job allowed Prevost to help shape the future of the Catholic Church.

The pope also named Prevost the president of the Pontifical Commission for Latin America. The job required Prevost to keep in close contact with Church leaders in that region. Pope Francis further honored Prevost by making him a cardinal, the rank within the Church just below the pope.

Prevost settled into his office in the Vatican, which seemed worlds away from his humble lodgings in Chiclayo. But he shied away from the social events attended by other Vatican officials as they competed with one another for power and influence. Prevost lived quietly in a small apartment near the Vatican. He refused the perk of having a nun take care of his housekeeping. He did his own shopping and cooking, although he often shared simple meals with Augustinian friends at St. Monica.

Prevost found selecting new bishops challenging. He pored over information about the candidates to look for the best possible leaders for the Church. Prevost wanted to find bishops who shared his and Pope Francis's commitment to the economically disadvantaged. He also searched for candidates who were as active in their communities as he had been in Peru.

At a press briefing in 2024, Prevost explained, "The bishop is not supposed to be a little prince sitting in his kingdom, but rather called authentically to be humble, to be close to the people he serves, to walk with them, to suffer with them."

Another goal for Prevost was increasing the size of the Catholic Church. "Our work is to enlarge the tent and to let everyone know they are welcome inside the Church," he said.

Prevost also used his position to call for stronger measures to combat climate change. He spoke at a conference in Rome that was attended by cardinals and climate experts. He called on them to do more to protect vulnerable environments, like those he had known in Peru.

Prevost (*right*) becoming a cardinal in 2023

Both Pope Francis and Prevost opposed allowing women in the priesthood. But Prevost did support the pope's efforts to provide women with greater leadership roles in the Church. Prevost had several women attend and vote at meetings to determine which bishop nominations he should recommend to the pope.

In 2024 Prevost came under fire for his handling of abuse allegations. Three Peruvian sisters went public in 2022 and said that two priests had abused them when they were children. They said they had told Prevost what happened, but he had failed to fully investigate the matter.

Prevost attends an event at a church in Illinois in 2024.

Prevost defended himself by pointing out the Church's official account of his actions. The Church explained that he first told the women to report the charges to the police. He then followed up with a report about their charges to the Vatican. Paola Ugaz, a reporter who investigated abuse in the Catholic Church, said, "Maybe he didn't do enough, but there was never any cover-up."

Prevost was more active in bringing to light Ugaz's investigation of Sodalitium Christianae Vitae, a Catholic sect in Peru. The reporter found evidence of abuse within its ranks. As a cardinal, Prevost removed a bishop associated with the group. He also persuaded Pope Francis to sever the Church's ties to the group.

The Conclave

Shutting down Sodalitium Christianae Vitae was one of Pope Francis's final acts. After being hospitalized with a lung infection, Pope Francis died on April 21, 2025, the day after Easter Sunday. Cardinals from around the world attended the pope's funeral. After the end of the formal mourning period, they turned their attention to holding a conclave to select the next pope.

During the preparation, the press made predications about who the College of Cardinals would choose. The clear choice was Pietro Parolin. He was the highest-ranking cardinal and had served as secretary of state for the Vatican under Pope Francis. Another option was

The funeral of Pope Francis was held on April 26, 2025.

Péter Erdő, a cardinal from Hungary. He was the favorite among the more conservative members of the College of Cardinals.

Prevost was also mentioned in many rundowns of candidates, although his election was seen as unlikely. The day before the conclave, his brother John called him and said he thought Prevost had a chance at becoming the first American pope. Prevost brushed off the idea, insisting he would not be selected. He believed the cardinals would never elect an American pope because Church leaders thought the United States was already too powerful in world affairs.

People watch a viewing of the cardinals entering the Sistine Chapel to begin the conclave in 2025.

On the evening of Wednesday, May 7, the cardinals formed a long procession as they entered the Sistine Chapel to begin the conclave. That night Parolin oversaw the first vote. As many people expected, Parolin had a good showing with more than 40 out of 133 votes. Two other cardinals also had high vote tallies—Erdő and Prevost.

After the conclave ended for the night, the cardinals retired for dinner and, more important, discussions about the leading candidates. Conversations showed that cardinals in North and South America strongly favored Prevost. Because he was an American and a Peruvian, both continents claimed him as one of their own.

Cardinals who did not know Prevost well began talking with cardinals who did. Many were impressed when they learned about his qualifications. Prevost had worked closely with parishioners, studied canon law, managed a religious order, traveled the world, and negotiated the internal politics of the Vatican. He also could speak French and Portuguese in addition to being fluent in English, Spanish, and Italian. His language skills meant that he could communicate with most of the cardinals in their native tongues.

Cardinals who knew Prevost also spoke highly of his personal qualities. He was easy to work with; had a quiet, calm manner; and was a skilled manager. He always listened to other people's ideas but had no trouble making decisions. More conservative cardinals were assured that even if they did not agree with Prevost on many policies, they would be able to work with him. Prevost tried to find a middle ground when people within the College of Cardinals disagreed.

The next morning, the second and third votes were held. Parolin's vote tally barely changed, but Prevost's began to grow. Many cardinals sensed the election shifting in Prevost's favor.

In the afternoon, during the fourth vote, Prevost began to breathe heavily as his name was read again and again. A cardinal sitting next to him gave him a piece of candy to calm his nerves. American Cardinal Joseph W. Tobin, a longtime friend of Prevost, said that when he cast his vote, "I took a look at Bob, and he had his head in his hands."

When Prevost's name was announced the eighty-ninth time, giving him two-thirds of the votes, he won the election. The cardinals rose to their feet and gave him a standing ovation. Only the stunned Prevost remained seated.

"Somebody had to pull him up," Cardinal Pablo Virgilio Siongco David of the Philippines said. "We were all teary-eyed."

As the highest-ranking cardinal, Parolin asked Prevost in Latin the question that has been posed to newly elected popes for centuries: "Do you accept your canonical election as the supreme pontiff?"

Prevost responded, "I accept."

A White Sox Fan

Pope Leo XIV has a favorite local sports team. Since he was a boy, he has been a fan of the White Sox baseball team. When the White Sox were in the 2005 World Series, he attended Game 1 at Chicago's U.S. Cellular Field, later renamed Guaranteed Rate Field. To celebrate one of the world's most famous White Sox fans, the stadium decorated a pillar with his image in May 2025 near the seat he sat in at the World Series.

Introducing Pope Leo XIV

The crowd gathered in St. Peter's Square cheered when the newly named Pope Leo XIV stepped onto the balcony of St. Peter's Basilica. But the audience for the event was far wider, as Catholics and others around the world watched Pope Leo XIV's first public address on computer, phone, and television screens. Many people, including world leaders and celebrities, immediately took to social media to express their congratulations and well-wishes to the new pope. Many also began searching for information about Pope Leo XIV and thinking about what his election would mean for the Catholic Church.

Pope Leo XIV speaks to the crowd from St. Peter's Basilica on May 8, 2025.

The image of Pope Leo XIV on the balcony provided some of the first clues. Around his shoulders he wore the traditional red cape with fur trim. Pope Francis, by contrast, had opted to wear plain white garments as a show of humility when he was named pope. Pope Leo XIV's clothing suggested he was not as eager to break with the past as Pope Francis had been, at least where the traditions of the Church were concerned. In his speech, however, Pope Leo XIV signaled that he would be as concerned with the economically disadvantaged as Pope Francis had been. He explained that he wanted to lead "a Church that always seeks peace, that always seeks charity, that always seeks to be close, especially to those who suffer."

In some ways, his speech highlighted ways his papacy might be unique. Like other popes, he initially spoke in Italian, but midway through his remarks, he switched to Spanish and spoke warmly of Chiclayo in Peru. The mention of his work in Chiclayo demonstrated the high value he placed on Catholic priests working in the service of everyday people. He did not speak in English or mention the United States. This suggested that he wanted the public to associate him more with his adopted country of Peru than with the nation of his birth.

His choice of the name Leo showed more of his priorities as pope. A Vatican spokesperson confirmed that he selected the name as a nod to Pope Leo XIII, who had served from 1878 to 1903. Pope Leo XIII had helped modernize the Church and championed workers' rights during the shift from agricultural to factory labor during the Industrial Revolution. Pope Leo XIV saw himself as leading the Church during a similar period. He wanted to protect workers, many of whose livelihoods could be threatened by artificial intelligence.

Other clues about Pope Leo XIV's reign came from his social media presence. Being on social media showed that he was in touch with contemporary life. Individual posts also revealed he was willing to confront world leaders about policies he believed went against Church teachings. In February 2025 he used the platform X to criticize President Donald Trump and Vice President JD Vance for deporting undocumented immigrants from the United States.

United States Secretary of State Marco Rubio (*left*) and United States Vice President JD Vance (*second from left*) meet with Pope Leo XIV on May 19, 2025.

The Challenges Ahead

On Sunday, May 18, 2025, Pope Leo XIV held his inaugural Mass, which was the symbolic beginning of his papacy. Heads of state and other foreign leaders came to the event to show their respect. Before a crowd of two hundred thousand people, Pope Leo XIV accepted two important symbols. One was a gold ring inscribed with his name and an image of Jesus's disciple Peter, who the Church considers to be the first pope. The other was a pallium, a ceremonial stole with a collar of lamb's wool, which symbolized that the pope guides his followers as a shepherd guides his flock.

At the beginning of his remarks in the inaugural Mass, Pope Leo XIV spoke of the "questions, concerns, and challenges of today's world." He was aware of the many challenges he would soon face. In his new role as pope, he would be called upon to help solve problems both within the Catholic Church and within the world at large.

One such problem was the tensions between conservative and progressive Church leaders. In some ways, Pope Francis's papacy had increased tensions as he worked to reform the Church. Conservatives had resisted his efforts to be more welcoming to the LGBTQIA+ community and to allow women to take on leadership roles. Although Pope Leo XIV was supportive of the previous pope's reforms, he was more traditional on those issues. His past stances suggested a willingness to negotiate compromises that both conservative and progressive cardinals could accept.

The Popemobile

For decades popes have traveled through public ceremonies on special vehicles called popemobiles. Many of these custom-made cars have been white and roofless. Inside they have often featured a raised platform so that the pope could be visible to the crowds that gather to see him. In 1981 Pope John Paul II was shot while he was riding in an open-air popemobile. He survived the event, but many later popemobiles were made with bulletproof glass. For his first popemobile ride, Pope Leo XIV chose an open-air version so he could better greet the public.

Pope Leo XIV waves to the crowd from a popemobile on May 18, 2025.

Another challenge was dealing with the abuse cases within the Church. Church officials, including Pope Leo XIV, had been accused of mishandling accusations by church members who had been abused by priests as children. One of Pope Leo XIV's first meetings was with Cardinal Seán Patrick O'Malley. O'Malley was the president of the Pontifical Commission for the Protection of Minors. The meeting signaled that openly dealing with the Church's abuse cases was a main goal of Pope Leo XIV's papacy.

Another concern for Pope Leo XIV was improving the Vatican's finances, which were running short by $94 million in 2025. The Church's fund to support retired Church employees also had far too little money in it. The cardinals had selected Pope Leo XIV in part because they thought his management experience could help him relieve the Vatican's financial problems. They also hoped that an American pope could convince wealthy Catholic Americans to donate more money to the Vatican.

The pope has world influence as a moral leader. The position could allow Pope Leo XIV to bring more attention to several international crises that concern him. These include inaction on climate change and the threats to human thriving posed by technologies such as artificial intelligence and social media. The pope has also long been an advocate for the humane treatment of migrant populations across the globe.

Another international threat that worries Pope Leo XIV is violent conflicts that have engulfed many nations. "In

Pope Leo XIV speaking during his inaugural Mass on May 18, 2025

this our time," Pope Leo XIV said at his inaugural Mass, "we still see too much discord, too many wounds caused by hatred, violence, prejudice." But as he concluded his address, the new pope offered a moving message of hope for a better future. He counseled not only his devout Catholic followers but all the people of the world to embrace love and unity.

"Together, as one people, as brothers and sisters," Pope Leo XIV said, "let us walk toward God and love one another."

IMPORTANT DATES

1955 Robert Francis Prevost is born on September 14 in Chicago, Illinois.

1973 He graduates from St. Augustine Seminary High School in Holland, Michigan.

1977 He graduates from Villanova University with a degree in mathematics.

1982 In Rome, Italy, Prevost is ordained as a priest in the Augustinian Order.

1984 He receives a degree in canon law from the Pontifical University of St. Thomas Aquinas in Rome.

1985 He travels to Peru to become a missionary in the town of Chulucanas.

1987 He returns to Chicago to work at the headquarters of the Midwest Augustinians.

1988 He moves to the Peruvian city of Trujillo, where he serves as a parish priest, a professor of canon law, and a judge in a religious court.

1999 Prevost leaves Peru and returns to the United States to lead the Midwest Augustinians in Chicago.

2001 He is elected to his first of twelve years as the head of the Augustinian Order.

2004 Prevost meets Cardinal Archbishop Jorge Mario Bergoglio, who became Pope Francis in 2013.

2014 Pope Francis sends Prevost back to Peru to serve as the administrator of the Diocese of Chiclayo.

2015 Pope Francis promotes Prevost to bishop.

Prevost obtains dual citizenship in Peru and the United States.

2023 Pope Francis appoints Prevost to lead the Dicastery for Bishops and promotes him to cardinal.

2025 Prevost is elected pope on May 8 and takes the name Leo XIV.

SOURCE NOTES

8 Nicole Winfield, "New Pope Chosen, White Smoke from Sistine Chapel Signals," PBS News, May 8, 2025, https://www.pbs.org/newshour/world/new-pope-chosen-white-smoke-from-sistine-chapel-signals.

10 Alessandro Di Bussolo, "The Election of a Pope: From White Smoke to 'Habemus Papam,'" Vatican News, May 7, 2025, https://www.vaticannews.va/en/pope/news/2025-05/election-new-pope-white-smoke-sistine-chapel-habemus-papam.html.

11 "The American Pope," Pillar, May 8, 2025, https://www.pillarcatholic.com/p/the-american-pope.

15 Alex Perez and Meredith Deliso, "Destined to Be Pope: Brother Says Leo XIV Always Wanted to Be a Priest," *Good Morning America*, May 9, 2025, https://www.goodmorningamerica.com/news/story/destined-pope-brother-leo-xiv-wanted-priest-121617183.

25 Franklin Briceno and Nicole Winfield, Associated Press," Pope Leo XIV Had to Overcome the Taboo Against a U.S. Pontiff," PBS News, May 8, 2025, https://www.pbs.org/newshour/world/pope-leo-xiv-had-to-overcome-the-taboo-against-a-u-s-pontiff.

27–28 "Cardinal Prevost: 'A Bishop Is Called to Suffer with the People He Serves,'" posted by Vatican News, October 23, 2024, YouTube video, 1:06, https://www.youtube.com/watch?v=AVRu6DWxF-A.

28 Joshua McElwee, "Prevost, First US Pope, Supported Francis and Shunned Spotlight," Reuters, May 8, 2025, https://www.reuters.com/world/prevost-first-us-pope-supported-francis-shunned-spotlight-2025-05-08.

30 Tom Kington et al., "The Real Pope Leo XIV—By Those Who Knew Him in Rome, Chicago and Peru," *Sunday Times* (UK), May 9, 2025, https://www.thetimes.com/world/europe/article/pope-prevost-chicago-cardinal-d2bt2p38l.

34 Jason Horowitz et al., "How a Quiet American Cardinal Became Pope," *New York Times*, last modified May 12, 2025, https://www.nytimes.com/2025/05/11/world/europe/conclave-vote-pope-leo-robert-prevost.html.

34 Horowitz et al.

34 Stacy Meichtry et al., "How an American Cardinal Beat the Odds to Become Pope," *Wall Street Journal*, May 9, 2025, https://www.wsj.com/world/europe/pope-leo-xiv-conclave-election-robert-prevost-0eb0f255?st=DK8fa1&reflink=desktopwebshare_permalink.

36 Aryn Baker, "'Peace Be with You': Pope Leo XIV Steps onto the World Stage," *Time*, May 9, 2025, https://time.com/7283865/pope-leo-robert-prevost.

38 Pope Leo XIV, "Full Text: Pope Leo XIV's Homily at Inaugural Mass Beginning His Petrine Ministry," Catholic News Agency, May 18, 2025, https://www.catholicnewsagency.com/news/264191/full-text-pope-leo-xivs-homily-at-inaugural-mass-beginning-his-petrine-ministry.

40–41 Pope Leo XIV.

41 Pope Leo XIV.

SELECTED BIBLIOGRAPHY

Horowitz, Jason, Emma Bubola, Elizabeth Dias, and Patricia Mazzei. "How a Quiet American Cardinal Became Pope." *New York Times.* Last modified May 12, 2025. https://www.nytimes.com/2025/05/11/world/europe/conclave-vote-pope-leo-robert-prevost.html.

Horowitz, Jason, Julie Bosman, Elizabeth Dias, Ruth Graham, Simon Romero, and Mitra Taj. "Long Drives and Short Homilies: How Father Bob Became Pope Leo." *New York Times*, May 17, 2025. https://www.nytimes.com/2025/05/17/world/europe/robert-prevost-pope-leo-xiv.html.

Kington, Tom, Will Pavia, and Iñigo Alexander. "The Real Pope Leo XIV—By Those Who Knew Him in Rome, Chicago and Peru." *Sunday Times* (UK), May 9, 2025. https://www.thetimes.com/world/europe/article/pope-prevost-chicago-cardinal-d2bt2p38l.

Kruse, Michael, and Bill Duryea. "55 Things You Need to Know About the New Pope, Leo XIV." *Politico*, May 9, 2025. https://www.politico.com/news/magazine/2025/05/09/55-things-you-need-to-know-about-the-new-pope-leo-xiv-00338515.

Mazzei, Patricia, and Matthew Mpoke Bigg. "The Small, Tight-Knit Religious Order That Molded Pope Leo XIV." *New York Times*, May 13, 2025. https://www.nytimes.com/2025/05/13/world/europe/pope-leo-order-of-st-augustine.html.

Meichtry, Stacy, Margherita Stancati, Ian Lovett, and Marcus Walker. "How an American Cardinal Beat the Odds to Become Pope." *Wall Street Journal*, May 9, 2025. https://www.wsj.com/world/europe/pope-leo-xiv-conclave-election-robert-prevost-0eb0f255?st=DK8fa1&reflink=desktopwebshare_permalink.

Ostberg, René. "Leo XIV." *Encyclopedia Britannica*. Last modified June 24, 2025. https://www.britannica.com/biography/Leo-XIV.

Rahman, Khaleda. "Pope Leo's Five Biggest Challenges." *Newsweek*, May 9, 2025. https://www.newsweek.com/pope-leo-biggest-challenges-2070204.

Schneid, Rebecca. "The Biggest Challenges Pope Leo XIV Faces." *Time*. Last modified May 8, 2025. https://time.com/7283867/pope-leo-challenges-diversity-globalization.

Taj, Mitra, Julie Turkewitz, and Genevieve Glatsky. "In Chiclayo, Peru, Locals Cheer the 'Peruvian Pope.'" *New York Times*, May 9, 2025. https://www.nytimes.com/2025/05/09/world/europe/pope-peru-reaction.html.

LEARN MORE

Andrews, Elizabeth. *Christianity*. DiscoverRoo, 2024.

Britannica Kids: Leo XIV
https://kids.britannica.com/students/article/Leo-XIV/648106

Britannica Kids: Roman Catholicism
https://kids.britannica.com/students/article/Roman-Catholicism/276778

Doeden, Matt. *Travel to Italy*. Lerner Publications, 2023.

Hamm, Liana. *A Look at Christianity*. BrightPoint, 2024.

The Holy See
https://www.vatican.va/content/vatican/en.html

INDEX

PHOTO ACKNOWLEDGMENTS

Image credits: Vatican Media/Abaca/Sipa via AP Images, p. 2; Rocco Spaziani/Archivio Rocco Spaziani/Mondadori Portfolio via Getty Images, p. 6; Marco Iacobucci Epp/Shutterstock, pp. 8, 31; Vatican Media/Getty Images, p. 9; Antonio Masiello/Getty Images, p. 11; Stefano Spaziani/Europa Press via Getty Images, pp. 12, 35; ARCHIVIO GBB/Alamy, pp. 14, 18; Wikimedia Commons PD, p. 16; Christian Vinces/Shutterstock, p. 20; STEFFANO PALOMINO/AFP via Getty Images, p. 21; R. Siciliani/Vatican Media/Sintesi/Alamy Live News, p. 24; AP Photo/Julio Reano, p. 26; Riccardo De Luca/Shutterstock, p. 28; courtesy of the Midwest Augustinian Province of Our Mother of Good Counsel, p. 29; ANDREAS SOLARO/AFP via Getty Image, p. 32; Simone Risoluti Vatican Media via Getty Images, p. 37; David Ramos/Getty Images, p. 39; Franco Origlia/Getty Images, p. 41. Design element: MirageC/Getty Images.

Cover image: Marco Di Lauro/Getty Images.